LEARN THE ALPHABETS

THROUGH FRUITS AND VEGETABLES
by
MINNIE DIX
Illustrated by Reverend Sheila Neal

Dedication

This book is dedicated to my parents
E. W. & Ruby Dix

This dedication is extended to
A'Mia McKenzie McKnight, DaQuan Tyrell Bells, Elijah Dix,
I-Beautiful Turner, Nevaeh Reynolds, Raheem Davis, Korreigh
Trinity Haskins, Jaliel Davis, Knowledge Michael Chapman,
Kayden Davis, Maddison Amonia Milligan, Kelsey Elise Prezzy,
Maddilyn Amiya Milligan and all the other boys and girls of
the world.

Acknowledgements

Dix, McKnight, Williams, Turner, Reynolds, Bells, Bookhardt,
Jones, McKune, Bennett, Greer, Rembert, Favor, Henderson,
Jenkins, Prince, Houck, Shuler, Murphy, Dash, Hamilton,
Johnson, Gordon, Richburg, Fairey, Fludd, Zeigler, Kennerly,
Frederick, Noah Frederick & Aidan Frederick, Clarkson, Barnett,
Pendleton and Morton.

Author's Note

This book is designed to teach children the alphabets through fruits and vegetables.

ILLUSTRATIONS BY REV. SHELIA NEAL
BOOK DESIGNED AND PUBLISHED BY MIRIKA CORNELIUS - AN AKIRIM PRESS PUBLISHING
ISBN 978-1-7333013-0-5

To visit author's website:
www.mcknightdixcreations.weebly.com.

Aa

apple

A

a

A is for apple and it is a fruit. It is good and healthy to eat.

Bb

banana

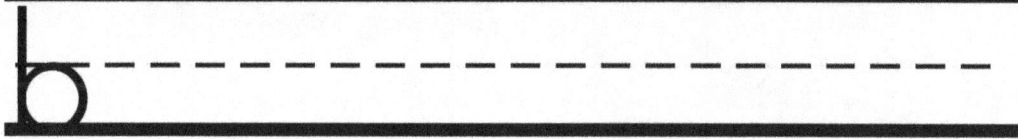

B is for BANANA. It is also a fruit. It is healthy and it can help protect your heart.

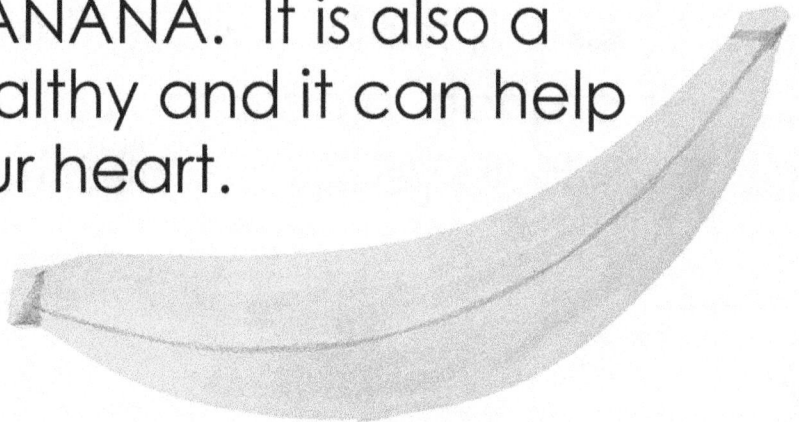

Cc

carrot

C is for CARROT. It is a vegetable. It is orange in color, full of vitamins and it will help you grow healthy and strong.

Dd

date

D is for DATE. It is a fruit that has healthy benefits for your body and is often eaten as a snack.

Ee

eggplant

E

e

E is for EGGPLANT. It is a fruit that is thought of as a vegetable. This fruit contains fiber, vitamins and minerals that are good for you.

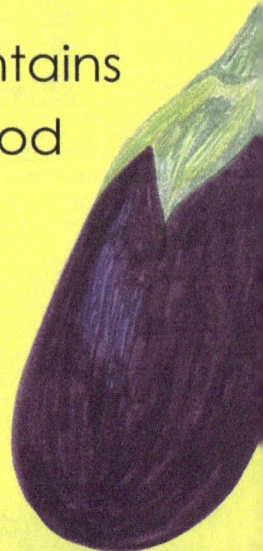

Ff

fig

F

f

F is for FIG. It is a fruit but it is often thought of as a vegetable. This fruit is delicious and it contains minerals and vitamins that are good for your body.

Gg

grapes

G -

g -

G is for GRAPE. It is a fruit. GRAPES are good for us. They are plump, juicy and the darker GRAPES are very healthy.

Hh

honeydew melon

H

h

H is for HONEYDEW. It is a fruit that belongs in the melon family. This fruit has lots of vitamins and minerals and can help keep your body healthy.

I i

irish potato

I is for IRISH POTATO. It is a vegetable. It is also known as a white potato. This vegetable contains fiber, vitamins and potassium, and it can help to keep your heart health.

Jj

jujube

J

J

j

j

J

is for JUJUBE. It is a fruit that is rich in minerals and vitamins that can help you maintain a healthy body.

Kk

kiwi

K -

k -

K is for KIWI. This is a fruit. KIWI is a nutritious fruit that tastes good. It contains vitamins and minerals that are helpful for your skin and it will help keep your body healthy and strong.

Ll

lettuce

L is for LETTUCE. This is a leafy vegetable. It contains vitamins and iron. LETTUCE helps to hydrate your body. It strengthens your bones and it helps you to stay healthy.

Mm

mushroom

M

m

M is for MUSHROOM. It is a vegetable. MUSHROOM is a healthy food that packs a nutritional punch that is good for you.

Nn

nectarine

N

n

N is for NECTARINE. This is a fruit. It has many healthy benefits. NECTARINE is a delicious fruit that can improve your immune system.

Oo

okra

O is for OKRA. This is a fruit. It is often cooked and eaten as a vegetable. OKRA has a great source of vitamins and nutrients to help you grow big and strong.

P p

pear

P -

p -

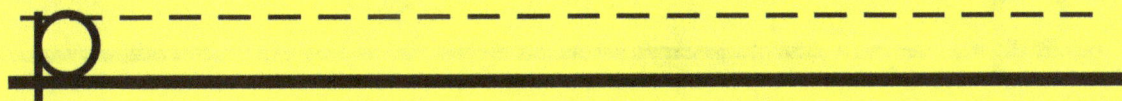

P is for PEAR. This is a fruit. PEAR is a juicy, enjoyable, fruit that contains vitamins, potassium and copper, and it is good for your body.

Qq

quince

Q

q

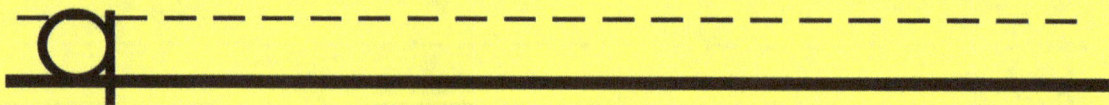

Q is for QUINCE. QUINCE is a fruit. It is rich in nutrients such as iron, potassium and vitamins to help keep your body healthy and strong.

Rr

radish

R

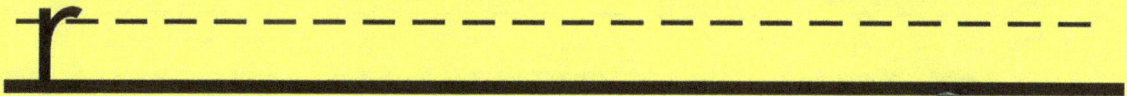

r

R is for RADISH. This is a vegetable that has a good source of vitamins but it should be eaten in moderation.

Ss

strawberry

S

S

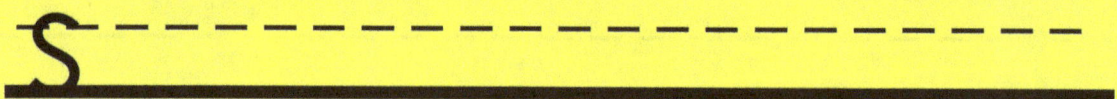

S is for STRAWBERRY. This is a fruit. STRAWBERRY is a fruit that is packed with potassium, vitamins and fiber. It is red, it is juicy and it is delicious.

Tt

tomato

T is for TOMATO. This is a fruit and a vegetable, but it is more often used as a vegetable. TOMATO has a source of vitamins and minerals that are good for you.

U u

ugli

U

U

U is for UGLI. UGLI is a fruit. This fruit is packed with healthy benefits that are good for your body, such as protein, iron, calcium and vitamins that will help you grow big and strong.

Vv

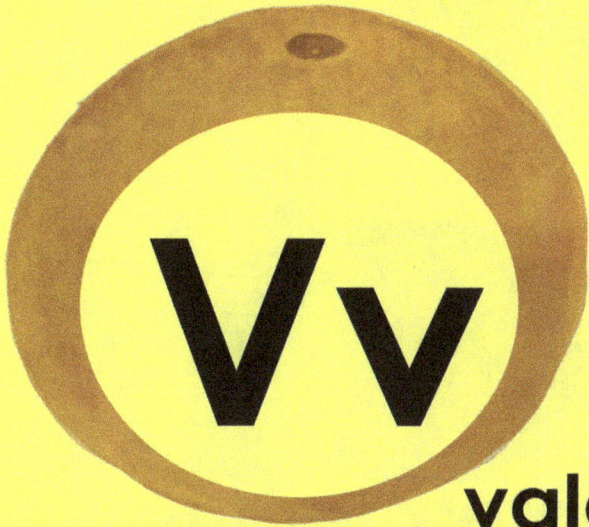

valencia orange

V

v

V

V is for VALENCIA ORANGE. This is a fruit. VALENCIA ORANGE is plump, tasty and it is good for you. It contains many nutrients, fiber and a high content of Vitamin C.

W w

watermelon

W

w

W is for WATERMELON. This is a fruit, a very healthy fruit. WATERMELON is sweet, delicious and it is packed with water that will help you maintain good health and good hydration.

Xx

xigua

X

x

X is for XIGUA. It is pronounced 'she gwah.' XIGUA is a fruit like a watermelon and it has some of the same healthy benefits, such as water.

Yy

yumberry

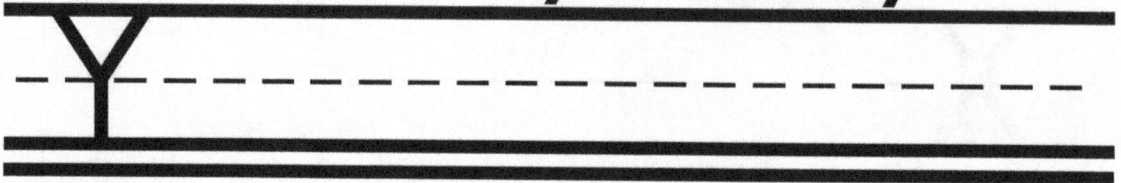

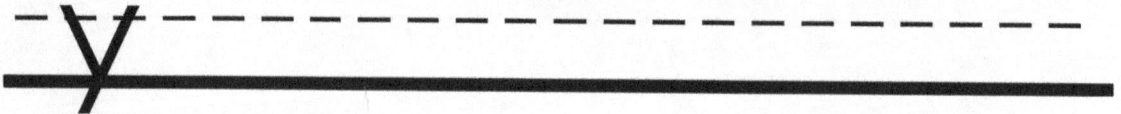

Y is for YUMBERRY. YUMBERRY is a small, maroon colored fruit and it is shaped like a grape. It is a healthy fruit that is good for digestion and it treats infections.

Zz

zucchini

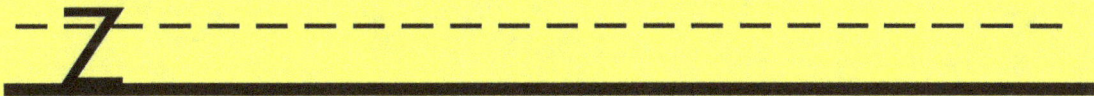

Z is for ZUCCHINI. ZUCCHINI is a fruit that is often thought of as a vegetable. ZUCCHINI has lots of healthy benefits such as protein, vitamins and calcium.

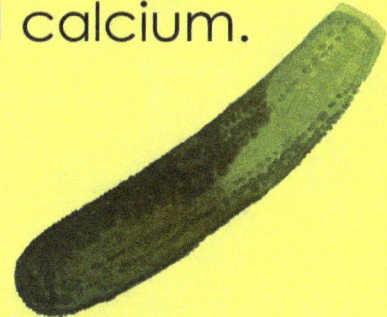

www.ingramcontent.com/pod-product-compliance
Lightning Source LLC
Chambersburg PA
CBHW050633150426

42811CB00052B/779